Copyright© 2016 by: Jeanne E. Rogers

All rights reserved. No part of this book may be reproduced or transmitted in any form or by any means without written permission from the author.

Published, 2016   ISBN-10 0-9907512-2-8

ISBN-13 978-0-9907512-2-9

Book design and illustrations by: Guy Atherfold - www.guyatherfold.co.uk

A CHILD'S ENVIRONMENTAL FABLE

J.E. Rogers

Illustrated by Guy Atherfold

For my father,
Sebastian Silvio Giacolano

*Thank you for your
love and guidance.*

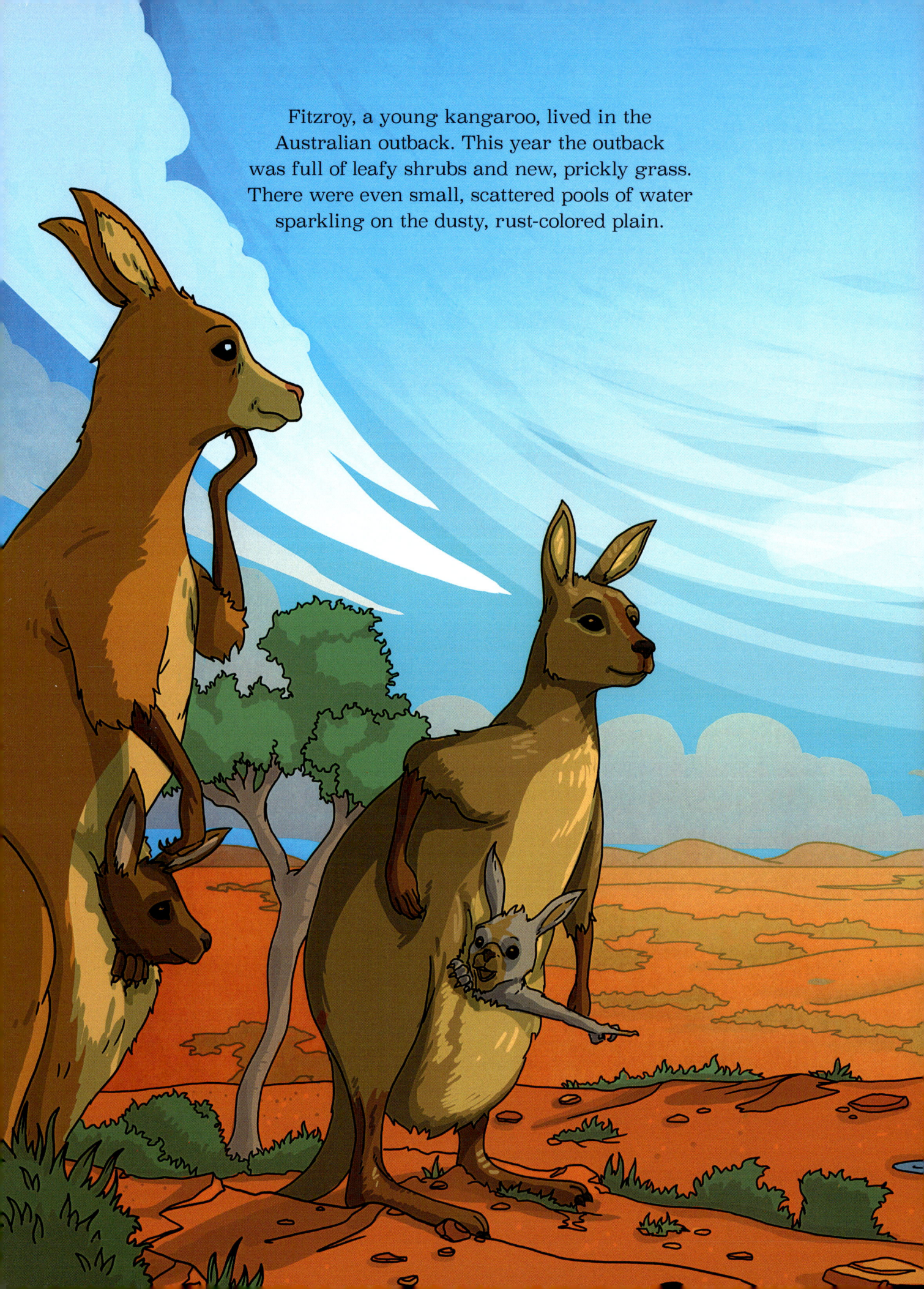

Fitzroy, a young kangaroo, lived in the Australian outback. This year the outback was full of leafy shrubs and new, prickly grass. There were even small, scattered pools of water sparkling on the dusty, rust-colored plain.

His kangaroo mob would enjoy the splendid view much more, if it weren't for the garbage pile sitting near the train tracks.

"It's because it rained," Fitzroy said. He wiggled a bit to make himself comfy in his mother's pouch.

"What's because it rained?" his friend Toby asked from a nearby pouch.

"Everything is greener because it rained," Fitzroy answered.

"Yeah, so what? Don't you ever pay attention to what's really important?" Toby asked. "Just look at that!"

The large pile of garbage by the train tracks was growing bigger by the day. Worse yet, its stench made some of the older roos and many of the younger joeys feel sick.

"You're right, Toby," Fitzroy admitted. "The green would be better if that stink wasn't there."

The mob had been discussing the pile for days, and no one had come up with a good idea for getting rid of it. Even Boomer, their leader and Fitzroy's dad, was bewildered.

"The outback would be just beautiful," Boomer said, "if it weren't for that rubbish down there."

"Dad?" Fitzroy peered up at his father.

"Yes, Fitzroy?" Boomer asked.

"We need to do something about it."

"You're right, son," Boomer replied.

"I have an idea," Fitzroy said excitedly.
"Why don't we call on the wedge-tailed eagles?
They'll help get rid of it. After all, they are scavengers."

"Fitzroy, that's a great idea!" Boomer turned to the mob and straightened up, making himself appear taller and more leader-like. "I think we should call on the wedge-tailed eagles," he announced. "They're a bunch of scavengers. They'll clean up that pile of garbage." Boomer waved to Darwin. Darwin was the strongest bounder in the group. "Darwin, get a message to the eagles. Tell them we need them here as soon as possible."

"Will do, sir."
Darwin saluted and bounded off in a northerly direction.

"Listen! Something's coming down the tracks!" exclaimed Fitzroy.

Sure enough, on the horizon, a black spot was growing bigger and bigger and the ground shook harder and harder.

"It's the train," Boomer shouted.

The rumbling of the train became a thunderous noise as the engine whizzed by with many passenger cars trailing behind. And then—like every other day—a window opened on one of the cars and a bag flew out. It hit the ground with a smack! The bag broke open and its contents exploded, right beside the rest of the garbage.

"Oh, my," Fitzroy's mother groaned. "That pile is growing bigger by the day."

A red cloud of dust billowed off the back of the train as it disappeared into the distance.

Soon, the wedge-tailed eagles arrived, and with a flutter of wings they landed above the mob in the branches of the ghost gum tree. Boomer stepped forward, looked up into the trees and greeted Murrin, the eagle king. Murrin bowed before the kangaroo leader, then darted his dark eyes from one kangaroo to the other.

"What, may I ask, is the emergency, Boomer?"

"Do you see that mountain of trash down there?" Boomer pointed a claw at the stinky pile that was growing alongside the train tracks. "We'd like to ask for your help in cleaning it up. We were hoping, since you and your boys are scavengers, you would consider carrying it away."

"I see." Murrin studied the pile of garbage, and said, "As you are well aware, Boomer, my mates and I are indeed scavengers. However, we did not create that mess and we will not be responsible for it."

"But, Murrin..." No sooner had the words slipped from Boomer's lips than the eagles were in flight.

"Now what?" Boomer murmured to himself.

"Dad!" said Fitzroy.

"Yes, Fitzroy?"

"I have an idea. Why don't we ask the dibblers? They have sharp teeth and sharp claws. They can rip up that mess in no time."

"Fitzroy, that's a great idea!" Boomer turned to the mob. "I think we should call on the dibblers," he announced. "They can bite and tear things with their sharp teeth and claws. They'll help clean it up." Boomer waved to Darwin. "Darwin, get a message to the dibblers. Tell them we need them here as soon as possible."

"Will do, sir." Darwin saluted and bounded off in a southerly direction.

It wasn't long before a troop of dibblers showed up. Their pointed noses sniffed the air and their black eyes sparkled.

"How ya doin', Boomer?" a large male dibbler named Bernard asked, as he stepped forward.

"We have a problem," Boomer said. "You see that?" Boomer pointed a claw at the steaming pile of garbage alongside the train tracks. "We'd like to ask your help in cleaning up that mess. We were hoping that you and your family, with your sharp claws and teeth, would consider clearing it away."

"Whoa! That's a tall order," Bernard said. "I don't believe we can help you out there, mate." The dibbler peered into Boomer's eyes. "Guess you didn't hear about the incident."

"What incident?" Boomer asked.

"Well, it was about three weeks ago. Uncle Alistair had been feeling a bit hungry all day and decided there might be something good to eat down in that pile." Bernard hesitated a moment, and tears filled his eyes. "We told him not to go. We told him it was too dangerous, but he didn't listen." He wiped the tears away. "We haven't seen him since. We can't help you. That is not our mess."

"But, but..." The dibblers began scurrying away before Boomer could finish his sentence. "Now what?" he murmured to himself.

"Dad!" Fitzroy said.

"Yes, Fitzroy?"

"Why don't we ask the camels?" Fitzroy suggested with a smile. "They are very good at hauling stuff. They can take it away."

"Fitzroy, that's a great idea!" Boomer turned to the mob. "I think we should call on the camels," he announced. "They're good at hauling stuff. We'll ask them to take that garbage away." Boomer waved to Darwin. "Darwin, get a message to the camels. Tell them we need them here as soon as possible."

"Will do, sir." Darwin saluted and bounded off in an easterly direction.

It wasn't long before a herd of camels lumbered over the soft red hills of the outback. Badu, the lead camel, strolled at the front of the herd.

"I say, ole' chap, how goes it?" Badu asked.

"Not bad, not bad," Boomer said, trying to sound positive. "We do, however, have a bit of a problem, and we thought you and your family could help us out."

"My good man, what might the problem be?"
Badu bent his neck downward so he could look into Boomer's eyes.

"Well, do you see that?" Boomer pointed a claw at the garbage pile that was growing alongside the train tracks. "We'd like to ask your help in clearing it up. You and your herd are excellent at hauling stuff. We were hoping that you would consider hauling it away."

Badu stared at the garbage pile. "I say!" Badu's eyes snapped open. "I do believe that's the most atrocious sight I have ever laid eyes on. It's true, we were good haulers once, but that mess is not ours. You must deal with that disgusting matter on your own!"

"But, Badu..." The camels turned, lifted their large flat feet and walked slowly away before Boomer could finish his sentence. "Now what?" he murmured to himself.

By this time, Darwin had become frustrated and a wee bit angry. He had traveled to the north to get the wedge-tailed eagles. He had traveled to the south to find the dibblers, and he had traveled to the east to find the camels.

"It has become painfully obvious to me," Darwin began, "that even if I traveled to the four corners of this great outback of ours that I would still not find anyone who would help us. Why don't we just pick up that garbage and throw it back at the people on the train?"

"That's right, mate," said one kangaroo. "Why don't we do that?"

"Yes, I agree," shouted another.

"Now, now," Boomer said calmly. "You're right, Darwin, but that won't do us any good." He had become more determined than ever. "We must take care of this problem on our own. After all, we live here, we raise our youngsters here, the land is ours and the mess is not healthy. It doesn't matter anymore whose mess it is."

"What do we need to do, Dad?" Fitzroy said.

"We must stand together, son."

"We will need to be brave. Right?"

"That's right, Fitzroy," Boomer nodded gravely. "And we must take responsibility."

There was a low chatter among members of the mob as Boomer walked courageously toward the train tracks. Without hesitation, the mob followed. Boomer positioned himself in the center of the tracks and all the kangaroos stood right there with him. The sound of the oncoming train was now in their ears. On the horizon, a black spot was growing bigger and bigger and the ground shook harder and harder.

The rumbling turned into a thunderous noise as the train came closer and closer. Its whistle screamed into the sky and Fitzroy curled deeper into his mother's pouch. The passengers on the train, noticing the mob on the tracks, hung out the windows and started waving and yelling at the kangaroos. The conductor shouted from the window of the train's engine. Then he pulled back hard on the brakes. At the last moment, the train came to a screeching halt just a few feet in front of the kangaroos.

Fitzroy peeked hesitantly out of his mother's pouch.

The conductor was infuriated with the kangaroos, and the passengers began to throw garbage at them. A banana peel landed on Fitzroy's brow and he hopped from his mother's pouch and looked at the train. There, in the window of one of the passenger cars, he saw a face. A small boy was staring down at him. Then the face disappeared and reappeared on the steps of the train.

Hopping down to the ground, the boy walked up to Fitzroy.
"Hi," the little boy said. "My name is Maxwell."

Fitzroy cocked his head and the banana peel fell to the ground.

"Stay away from those dirty animals," an angry woman shouted from an open window. Other voices joined that of the woman, and many of the passengers were shaking their fists at the kangaroos. But the screams and taunts did not move Boomer or his mob. They stood their ground.

Maxwell looked down at the banana peel that had fallen from Fitzroy's head to the red, dusty earth. "I think you and your family need help," he said.

Fitzroy nodded.

"This…this is not your mess, is it?" Maxwell asked.

The boy's father appeared on the steps of the passenger car.
"Get back in here, Maxwell. Don't go near that animal!"

Maxwell looked between his furious father, the angry travelers hanging from the windows of the passenger cars, and the kangaroo mob, which was still blocking the tracks. To the astonishment of everyone, including the kangaroos, Maxwell bent down and picked up the banana peel from the ground and put it in his pocket. Turning to Fitzroy, Maxwell smiled, nodded and the young joey nodded back. Together, in silent understanding, Fitzroy and Maxwell began picking up the garbage. As Fitzroy lifted a cardboard box, Uncle Alistair crawled out from underneath it.

"Thank you!" he said, wiping dust from his snout. "I thought I'd never be found." The old dibbler let out a joyous squeak as he scampered away.

Soon a little girl stepped off the train with a box, and she began filling the box with rubbish. Then a few teenage boys did the same. Soon many other passengers joined in and filled as many containers as they could. Slowly, the mess was being cleared away from beside the tracks.

Boomer waved to his mob. "Let's go. We can all help."
Soon all the roos were lending a paw.

When the garbage was finally cleaned up, the passengers put all the boxes and bags of rubbish on board and climbed back on the train.

Maxwell wrapped his arm around Fitzroy's shoulders and said, "You didn't make this mess, and I didn't make it either. But people did, and I am so sorry for that." He looked out across the glittering, green outback and a huge smile lit his face. "I will remember this day," Maxwell said. "I think we all will. We have learned a lot about responsibility and taking care of the land, even if we don't live here." Maxwell stepped back and said, "We will do our best to make sure this does not happen again." The boy waved goodbye as he boarded the passenger car. The mob moved off the track, and the train rolled slowly forward. The passengers leaned out the windows and waved goodbye.

As Fitzroy hopped back into his mother's pouch for a well-deserved nap, a cloud of red dust billowed off the train's caboose as it disappeared in a westerly direction.

ABOUT THE AUTHOR

Healesville Sanctuary, Melbourne, Australia

J.E. Rogers is a graduate of Western Connecticut State University. Infused with a reverence for life, she loves animals and has always been especially intrigued by the unusual wildlife that can only be found in Australia. An avid student of every facet of the country, Rogers' love of all things Australian has flowed into her books. She hopes to spark an interest in young readers to the flora and fauna of the Land Down Under, while engaging them in a wildly imaginative tale of adventure.

J.E. Rogers is dedicated to teaching youngsters, at libraries, schools, and museums, about endangered and threatened animals around the globe. She wants children to understand that we are connected with all life on this planet, that animals are our fellow creatures and we share this world with them. It is our responsibility to protect them for ourselves and for future generations.

Other books by J.E. Rogers:

The Sword of Demelza

The Gift of Sunderland

Find J.E. Rogers at:

warriorechidna.blogspot.com

facebook.com/australianfantasyadventures

Or send an email to her at: Jeanne.rogers22@gmail.com

GLOSSARY

AUSTRALIA

Australia is an island country and the smallest of the seven continents. There are more than twenty million people living in Australia, a mere fraction of the population of the United States. A great majority of the country is desert, located in the central portion. Most of the population lives on the coasts.

CAMEL

There are approximately one million wild camels in Australia, the largest camel population in the world. Thousands were imported to Australia in the 19th century to be used for transportation, and once their use diminished, they were set free to roam in the outback. The majority of camels in The Outback are dromedaries, the one-humped species. Camels were important in the growth of Australia, as they helped people open up the dry outback, thus making those areas accessible.

To learn more about the dromedary camel, visit this site:
a-z-animals.com/animals/camel/

(Photo Credit: Author, via Shutterstock)

DIBBLER

This meat-eating marsupial, which looks much like a mouse, is one of the most endangered mammals on the planet. It is found almost exclusively on two islands off the southwestern portion of Australia, but it has also been seen in several of Australia's national parks and reserves. It is busy at dawn and dusk when it hunts small insects, lizards, and even birds.

To learn more about the dibbler, go to this site: **www.arkive.org/dibbler/ parantechinus-apicalis/**

(Photo Credit: Perth Zoo, Perth, Australia)

GHOST GUM TREE

Gum Tree is a general term that covers a number of different species of trees, including Eucalyptus trees, which Koala's love to eat. Most Gum Trees are found in Australia, but there are some that grow outside the country, as well. The Ghost Gum has an unusually white and smooth bark. They are especially beautiful on a moonlit night.

To learn more about gum trees, visit this site: **australia.gov.au/about-australia/ australian-story/eucalypts**

(Photo Credit: Author's collection.)

KANGAROO

There are more than forty species of Kangaroo, the red kangaroo being the largest. It is the biggest animal in the world that hops to get around, and is also the largest marsupial. Their back legs cannot move independently and they can leap up to thirty feet. Kangaroos are not endangered and are found throughout the arid regions of Australia. There are more than forty million kangaroos in Australia.

To learn more about kangaroos, visit this site:
www.arkive.org/red-kangaroo/macropus-rufus/

(Photo Credit: Author, via Shutterstock)

BOOMER

A male kangaroo is called a 'boomer,' a buck or an 'old man.' A female kangaroo is called a doe or a flyer

JOEY

A name for a baby kangaroo.

MARSUPIAL

A marsupial is a kind of mammal that has a pouch. Their babies are born in an immature state and mature inside their mothers' pouches while attached to her nipples. The babies stay inside their mothers' pouches for weeks or months, depending on the species.

To learn more about marsupials, visit this site:
www.ucmp.berkeley.edu/mammal/marsupial/marsupial.html

MOB

A large group of kangaroos is called a mob.

THE OUTBACK

"The Outback" is a general term that is used for any area of Australia that is sparsely populated. The term is synonymous with emptiness and remoteness, which describes the huge center of the continent. The Outback covers more than 2.5 million square miles. It is also referred to as 'the bush' to those who make it their home.

(Photo Credit: Author, via Shutterstock)

WEDGE-TAILED EAGLE

The Wedge-Tailed Eagle is the largest bird of prey in Australia and one of the largest eagles in the world. It is capable of soaring for hours on end without flapping its wings. Its diet consists of rabbits, wallabies, small kangaroos, swamp birds and reptiles. The name of this bird is derived from its long, diamond-shaped tail.

To learn more about the Wedge-Tailed Eagle, visit this site:
www.arkive.org/wedge-tailed-eagle/aquila-audax/

(Photo Credit: From the author's collection)